GOD: *the* ULTIMATE GARDENER

Created by
Blossom

GOD: THE ULTIMATE GARDENER

Published by
Come Grow with Me Books
www.comegrowwithmebooks.com

Book Formatting and Editing
DHBonner Virtual Solutions, LLC
www.dhbonner.net

ISBN: 979-8-9928784-0-0

Published in the United States of America

To my beloved Grandmother, Estelle G. Williams, who first placed my hands in the soil and planted within me a love for gardening. Your gentle guidance, love for Christ Jesus, and godly wisdom taught me that every seed holds a promise, just as God's Word does.

To my wonderful mother, Janice W. Howard, whose love, correction, prayers, and unwavering support have shaped me into the woman I am today. Your faith and strength have been my greatest example, reminding me that with God, all things grow in His perfect time.

To Pastor Dr. Eric Thomas (ET The Hip Hop Preacher), whose unwavering coaching, mentorship, guidance, and example of faith in action has helped me deepen my walk with God, strengthen my relationship with Him, and unlock a gift that I never knew I had. Through your encouragement, I have found my voice in writing, and for that, I am forever grateful.

May this book bless every child who reads it, nurturing in them a heart that trusts in God's seasons and a spirit that delights in His creation.

1

THE MARVELOUS GARDEN

Once upon a time, in a land of vibrant colors and endless beauty, there was a magnificent garden unlike any other. This garden was not just any garden... it was a creation of love, tended by the ultimate gardener, GOD.

2

SEEDS OF CREATION

In this beautiful garden, God planted seeds of every kind—tiny seed that held the promise of life. With a gentle touch and a loving heart, God sowed seeds of flowers, trees, and all sorts of fruit and vegetables. Each seed held a unique story, waiting to unfold.

3
NURTURING LOVE

Day by day, God watched over the garden, nurturing each plant with tender care. Like a loving parent, God provided all each plant needed: sunlight, rain, and the perfect soil for growth.

The garden flourished. A symphony of different colors, shapes, and scents all thrived and celebrated the creator's loving care. All the plants trusted God to meet their needs.

4

LESSONS FROM NATURE

As children explored the garden's nooks and crannies, they discovered valuable lessons hidden among the petals and leaves. They learned about patience from the slow opening of a flower bud and about courage from the tiny seedlings that pushed up through the soil as they searched for the light and reached for the sky.

5

SEASONS OF LIFE

The garden changes with the seasons, just as life does. In the spring, new life bursts forth with vibrant energy! Summer brings warmth and abundance! Autumn paints the leaves with a bright hue as a reminder that there is a season to shed the old and embrace the new. Winter comes as a season of rest and renewal—the soil rests and regenerates in preparation for spring.

6

THE GARDENER'S HELPERS

One day, the children met the gardener's friendly helpers-busy bees, fluttering butterflies, and industrious earthworms. They learned that these creatures, just like themselves, were part of God's grand design, and played a special part in the harmony of God's garden.

7

A GARDEN OF KINDNESS

Amid the flowers and laughter, the children discovered the magic of being kind. They realized, like God, they could nurture the world around them with love, compassion, and care. They realized that every act of kindness was like a drop of water, helping the garden called "Life" to flourish.

8

THE GARDEN'S SECRETS

One day, a wise old tree whispered a secret to the children. It told them that the garden was more than just a place of beauty. It was a reflection of God's love, and a living reminder that the Creator was always near, lovingly watching over all He had created, including them.

9

TENDING THE HEART'S GARDEN

With new-found understanding, the children returned to their own homes, carrying the lessons from the garden with them. They realized that just as God tended to the earth's garden, they could and should tend the garden of their hearts by cultivating kindness, joy, and love.

10

A BLOOMING FRIENDSHIP

As the seasons turned into years, the children grew into caring adults. They remembered the lessons they had learned from the ultimate gardener, God.

And, as they walked through life's garden,
they continued to plant seeds of hope, nurture
relationships, and bloom with the beauty of
a garden touched by God's hand. They also
remembered that God, their Creator,
considers them His friend too.

ABOUT THE AUTHOR

Andrea T. Howard is a Certified Master Gardener whose passion for gardening began as a seed lovingly planted and cultivated by her grandmother, Estelle G. Williams. Inspired by the beauty of God's creation and the lessons found in nature, Andrea weaves biblical truths into stories that help children grow in faith, patience, and perseverance—just like a well-tended garden.

With years of experience teaching and encouraging children in her church community, Andrea finds joy in nurturing young hearts through storytelling. When she's not in the garden, she enjoys bowling, traveling, and inspiring others to grow—both in life and in faith.

To connect with Andrea and explore more of her work, visit her website at **www.comegrowwithmebooks.com**, visit **"Come Grow with Me Books"** on Facebook and Instagram, or email her at **andrea@comegrowwithmebooks.com.**

Made in the USA
Columbia, SC
22 May 2025

58299512R00015